I See Fish

Written by Don L. Curry

SCHOLASTIC INC.

New York   Toronto   London   Auckland   Sydney
Mexico City   New Delhi   Hong Kong   Buenos Aires

Can you see fish?

I can see an orange fish.

I can see a blue fish.

I can see a red fish.

I can see a yellow fish.

I can see a green fish.

I can see a purple fish.

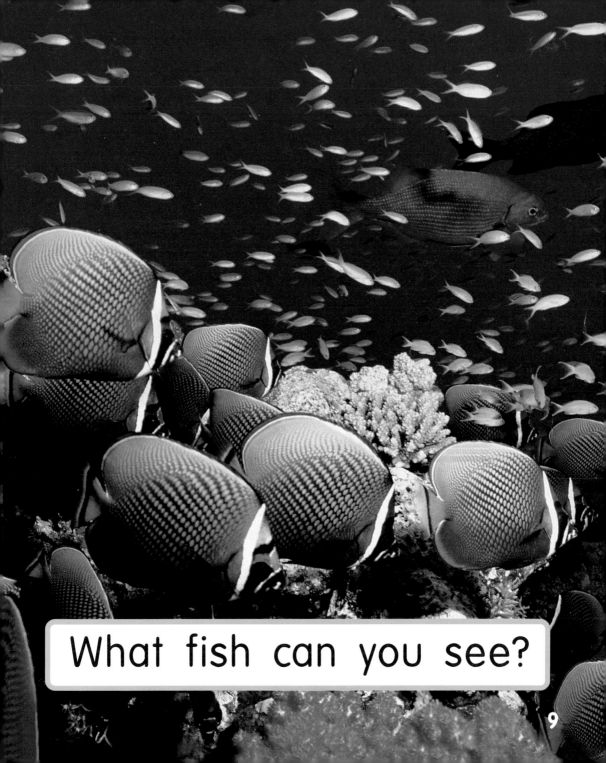

What fish can you see?

Photo Credits:

Front Cover: © Fred Bavendam/Peter Arnold, Inc.;
Title Page: © Fred Bavendam/Peter Arnold, Inc.;
p. 2: © Fred Bavendam/Peter Arnold, Inc.;
p. 3: © Dave Fleetham/Tom Stack & Associates;
p. 4: © Stephen Fink/CORBIS;
p. 5: © Fred Bavendam;
p. 6: © Dave Fleetham/Tom Stack & Associates;
p. 7: © W. Gregory Brown/Animals Animals;
p. 8: © Zigmund Leszczyski/Animals Animals;
p. 9: © Dorothy Cutter/Natural Selection;
Back Cover: © Fred Bavendam/Peter Arnold, Inc.

Copyright © 2002 by Scholastic Inc.
All rights reserved. Published by Scholastic Inc.
Printed in the U.S.A.

ISBN 0-439-45563-4

SCHOLASTIC and associated logos and designs are trademarks and/or registered trademarks of Scholastic Inc.

1 2 3 4 5 6 7 8 9 10   23   11 10 09 08 07 06 05 04 03 02